Chiengmai

Vientiane

LAOS

Gulf of Tonkin

VIETNAM

Hainan
(China)

THAILAND

Ping R.

Wang R.

Yom R.

Chao Phraya R.

Klong R.

Ayudhaya

Bangkok

Angkor

River

CAMBODIA

SOUTH VIETNAM

Mekong

Phnom
Penh

Saigon

Gulf of Thailand

Malay

Peninsula

South

MALAYA

THAILAND: RICE BOWL OF ASIA

takes you inside this lovely Oriental country, once the faraway Kingdom of Siam. Here is a fascinating introduction to this corner of Southeast Asia, now closer to Western doorsteps than ever before.

Glimpse the warm, easy pattern of Thai family life and meet people in bustling Bangkok, along quiet rice paddies, in forest lumber camps. Travel along the *klongs* with Thai children on their way to school and celebrate with them the gay holidays of *Tod Kathin* and the Buddhist New Year.

Here is the glamour of a colorful kingdom, the background for introductions to Thai history, geography, and government. Agriculture and industry, modern buildings and ancient temples are here to be explored.

This unique, fresh approach to elementary social studies is given new vividness by stories, some by a talented young Thai writer, and paintings by a young Thai artist trained both in old traditions and new ways.

Pictures by Thai artist Payut Ngaokrachang

THAILAND
RICE BOWL OF ASIA

By JANE WERNER WATSON

GARRARD PUBLISHING COMPANY   CHAMPAIGN, ILLINOIS

Acknowledgments

The author and publisher are grateful to Mr. Anand Panyarachun for checking the accuracy of this manuscript. Mr. Panyarachun is First Secretary, Permanent Mission of Thailand to the United Nations.

The paintings and drawings illustrating the stories in this book have been done especially for it by an able Thai artist, Payut Ngaokrachang.

The endsheet map of Thailand and its neighbors is by James A. Bier.

The stories, "A Happy, Damp New Year" and "The Golden Serpent Barge," are by Ramadi Vasnasong, a young Thai writer who lived in Washington, D. C. until she was six years old. Mrs. Vasnasong was also of invaluable assistance in acting as liaison between the artist and the author.

Photo credits

Caroline Porter Green, Pages 80, 81, 108
Permanent Mission of Thailand to the United Nations, Pages 47, 59, 91
P. I. P. Photos, Page 23
Royal Thai Embassy, Washington, D. C., Pages 27, 53
Tourist Office of Thailand, Page 59
United Nations, Pages 31, 43, 51
Wide World Photos, Pages 5, 90
Other photographs by the author

Cover Art by Payut Ngaokrachang

Contents

1. The Long Way Home

The small train chuffed to a stop. Anek picked up his bundle and jumped down. He waved his thanks to the driver. Then with his bundle over his shoulder, he walked off down the road. He whistled a happy tune as he went. Anek was going home.

For two years he had worked in the forests of south Thailand. Each day he had ridden his elephant down forest trails. With a touch of his heel or knee he had told Chang, the elephant,

5

what to do. Together they had rolled many a heavy log into place to be loaded on the small train. But now Anek was going home.

For a while he had wondered if he would get away. For Chang, the elephant, did not want him to go. An elephant does not like to have to train a new boy to look after him. When Anek said good-by, Chang snatched his red and black bundle and flung it as far as he could.

The lumber train was chuffing on the track. It could not wait. The bundle caught on the branch of a tree. Poor Anek! What could he do?

Men shouted. A boy climbed the tree. He threw down the bundle. Men tossed it from hand to hand, back to Anek.

Anek could hear Chang trumpeting unhappily. He saw Chang's head go down. His tusks pointed threateningly. Two of the *mahouts* rode their elephants close in beside him. They held Chang in place. So Anek was able to hop safely onto the small train to start his long journey home.

From the small village where the lumber train stopped, Anek got a ride to town in a bullock cart. In the town he found a red bus bound for Bangkok.

In Bangkok Anek would board a big, fast train to the north. Soon, after two long years away, Anek would be back home!

"I have gotten away from my elephant," Anek said to himself. "I have ridden on a lumber train, in an ox cart, and now on a bus. Only one simple train ride is left. Then I shall be back home."

Anek's bus traveled alongside a *klong,* or canal. Small boats darted about on the canal. Houses on the far side gazed at themselves in its mirror surface. They seemed to look up in surprise as the bus roared past. Perhaps they knew that Anek was going home.

After some time, there were more and more houses. Long rows of them, pushed together side by side, lined the road. There were shop fronts with bright windows. People hurried up and down. Cars and bicycles raced about. Horns honked. Whistles blew. Voices called out. This was Bangkok, the big, busy city of Thailand.

"How will I ever find the railway station in a big city like this?" Anek wondered as he stepped down from the bus with his bundle in his hand.

"Taxi?" said a voice beside him.

There at the curb stood a tiny three-wheeled car. The driver was smiling pleasantly. The small seat behind him was empty.

"If you can get me to the train to Chiengmai," (cheng-my) said Anek, "I will be going home."

"Going home, eh?" said the taxi driver. "Jump in. That train will leave soon."

Anek tossed his bundle onto the taxi seat. He jumped in beside it. Off they went, with a roar of the motor. They went so fast that Anek had to hold on with both hands. The black and red bundle slid from the seat. It slid across the floor. If it slid out, it would be lost under the wheels of a bus or truck! It had been saved from Chang, the elephant. Anek did not want to lose it now.

The taxi drew up in front of a long building. The bundle was still safe at Anek's feet. He sighed a deep sigh.

"Here you are," said the cheery driver. "Just inside that door you will find the ticket window. You have time to buy a ticket to Chiengmai."

Soon Anek was in line in front of the window. The floor was littered with suitcases and boxes and bundles. Anek set his bundle down. He counted out *bahts* for his ticket. (A *baht* is worth about five cents.) It took most of his savings to buy that ticket, for Chiengmai is at the northern end of the railway line.

"The train is ready on track four," said the ticket man.

As Anek tucked away his remaining money, he looked down at his bundle. It was not there! Suitcases, boxes, and bundles stood about by the dozens. But Anek's red and black bundle was nowhere to be seen!

"My bundle!" cried Anek.

He ran back to the station doorway, trying

to think. As he reached the doorway, a troop of boys ran by. They were throwing a bundle among them like a ball. The bundle was red and black. It was Anek's!

"Ho!" shouted Anek. He ran after the boys, out the station door.

"Young man!" the ticket man shouted after him. "You will miss your train to Chiengmai!"

But Anek ran on.

Up one street, across another ran the boys, still tossing the bundle. After them ran Anek.

The crowds thickened. Everyone seemed to be looking up, so Anek looked up too. At first he saw just the sharp-peaked roof of a temple. Then he saw the swing!

Giant posts painted bright red poked up against the sky. From a crossbar between them hung the giant swing. Four men sat on its seat. They waved to the people and did stunts as they swooped and dived through the air.

Over at one side was a long bamboo pole with a small sack of money at its tip. Soon the swingers would try to snatch the money sack with their teeth. This was a high point of the old Hindu festival.

10

Swish! Something sailed up against the sky. A man on the giant swing reached out and caught it. It was Anek's bundle! Before the whole crowd, he opened the bundle. He took out Anek's extra shirt and held it up. While the crowd laughed, he put it on over his own. He took out Anek's plaid headcloth and wrapped it around his head.

"This is great!" said a boy beside Anek. He and his friends were laughing heartily. "This bundle stunt is new."

"It is my bundle!" cried Anek. "And those are

11

my clothes. I was going home. Now I have lost
my clothes and I have missed my train."

"Someone took your bundle? What a shame!"
said the boys. "But *mai pen rai!* (my pen re)
Never mind! What does it matter? Come and
enjoy the festival with us."

Anek's new friends took him by the arm. They
led him off to the food sellers' stands. They got
him spicy chicken and a packet of rice. They
all had bottles of fruit drinks and coconut sweets.

Soon Anek was having a wonderful time. He forgot his lost bundle and the train which had long ago left for Chiengmai.

Night fell. Fireworks, purple and red and gold, flashed against the dark sky. Music sparkled up all around. With his new friends, Anek watched a puppet show. He saw some dancers sway and pose in beautiful costumes with strange masks on their heads. He watched a boxing match.

After a while the bands began to drift away. The last basketful of golden stars drifted down the sky. The crowds thinned.

"Let's go home," said the boys.

Home! Anek felt suddenly sad. He remembered his troubles again.

"You will come home with me," said one of the boys with a smile. "Tomorrow we will put you on the train to Chiengmai."

The boys kept their word. But before they took Anek to the station, they all went shopping.

"Our friends are sorry about what happened to your bundle," they said. "They want you to have a new set of clothes to remember us and Bangkok by."

With a new bundle full of clothes and presents for his family, Anek reached the station again. The train was ready on track four. On the long covered platform, girls were selling fruit, rice cakes, bananas, and soft drinks. Anek counted out some *bahts* from his savings and bought soft drinks and cakes for all his new friends. They found him a good seat on a wooden bench beside a window in one of the cars. They waited until the train pulled out, all waving good-by.

Anek watched the city slip away behind the train. He watched the *sampans,* small boats on the canals. He watched the boys on their water buffalo and the bigger boys playing ball beside the track after the day's work.

Soon green rice fields stretched away on all sides. The day began to fade. Darkness crept over the flat land. Lights flashed on in scattered houses. When Anek could not see outside any more, he turned away from the window to look around him in the car.

Beside him sat an old man with a thin white beard.

"At twilight we left Bangkok," the old man said. "Now we sit in our places, and tomorrow

14

morning we reach Chiengmai. Travel is not what it used to be. When I made my first trip down from Chiengmai, it took three months."

"Did you walk, Grandfather?" asked Anek.

"Ho!" laughed the old man. "No, we traveled down the river in those days. There were few railroads. There were few roads. The king and nobles had elephants to ride on land. But I traveled down the River Ping in a slender swallow-tailed boat. What a journey that was!

"Do you know the River Ping? It foams along between tall cliffs. Their stone walls are red and orange and green. They are carved by wind and water into fortresses and towers and deep dark caves. How we sang, as we rushed down those narrow gorges, to keep our spirits up!

"There are waterfalls, too, that thunder and roar. We had to unload the boat at the top of the falls and climb down a steep and slippery path to reload at the foot.

"There are rapids where the water foams into white clouds over rocks. We saw a boat smashed into matchsticks on those rocks. The boatmen vanished in the foam. Probably they had not made an offering to the evil spirits that live in the rocks!

"We made our offerings, you may be sure. Still, before reaching the worst of the rapids, we went ashore. We scrambled along the bank, pulling the empty boat."

When Anek drifted off to sleep, he dreamed of the foaming river. He dreamed of bounding boats and the shouts of boatmen as they leaned on long poles or oars.

Anek awoke in the gray dawn. Mist was rising in white swirls from canals and paddy fields. Above rose the dark green wall of the forest, brightened with the pale feathers of bamboo plants.

Beside the tracks, Anek saw teak logs lined up in rows to dry. That sight looked like home.

The train roared into a black tunnel. Out of
the blackness it chugged again into the sunny
morning. Far away Anek saw soft blue hills.
Those were the hills of his north country. They
were hills near Chiengmai!

The train stopped. There was no village in
sight. Only the neat houses of the railway
workers stood beside the tracks. But many village
people had come to meet the train. To Anek they
all looked like old friends. There were boys
carrying poles from which lottery tickets hung
like leaves on a tree. There were girls carrying
potted orchid plants in baskets hanging from
shoulder yokes. There were women holding up

trays of fruit, of peanuts, of spiced chicken, to the windows of the train. They called cheery greetings.

Anek bought two servings of rice, one for the old man and one for himself. It was the good sticky rice of the north. Anek had not had any of that in two years. Before they finished, the train started with a snort and a puff.

Soon Anek spotted a long, long flight of steps on a steep hillside beside the tracks. An old monk in an orange robe rested beside the steps. Anek's heart leaped. He knew those steps. He had climbed them, the whole thousand of them. He knew the temple at the top. In his heart he could hear its small bells tinkle in the breeze. Now he could not wait to be home once more!

"No," said the old man beside him, with a sigh. "Travel is not what it was in the old days. Swallowtail boats on the river, elephants on land—that was the way to go. There is no excitement left now."

"Traveling today suits me, Grandfather," smiled Anek. "We have had enough excitement, my bundle and I, on the long road home to Chiengmai."

CHINA

BURMA

LAOS

THAILAND

CAMBODIA

VIETNAM

GULF OF THAILAND

MALAYA

2. This is Thailand

Picture a well-fed Siamese cat, sleek and beautiful. Its back is sharply arched; its head is down. Now picture this sleek cat-figure on a map of southeast Asia. Its nose is tucked in between Cambodia and Laos on the east. Its spine arches up between Laos and northern Burma. Its back legs rest against Burma in the west. Its front paws curl around the Gulf of Thailand to the south. Its tail, strangely, stretches

21

out far below its hind feet, down the Malay Peninsula. This beautiful, well-fed "creature" is Thailand (tie-land). Until 1939, foreigners called it Siam.

Thailand's "tail and spine" are bony with hills and mountains that are covered with forests. Its "tail" reaches almost to the equator in the south. Its "belly" is soft with rich rice fields. Its "head" is a high, dry plain.

No such picture of a country can be really accurate. But this does give us a first glimpse of Thailand's geography.

Life-Giving Waters

Down from the hills in the north, sweep beautiful rivers. They cut their way through deep gorges. They plunge down falls. They foam over rapids.

When they reach the plain, these rivers from the north flow together into one great stream, the Menam Chao Phraya (may-nam chah-o pry-ah). Because it is the main artery of Thailand, this stream is known as Menam or The River.

The Menam and its tributaries have really

The plains of Thailand are a checkerboard of rice paddies. These workers are weeding the rice which, in three months, will be ready to harvest.

created much of modern Thailand. All the land of the central plain is mud which the rivers have carried down from the hills in the north. This wide flat plain is cut into a checkerboard by countless canals called *klongs,* the main highways of the country.

Rain and Rice

Over most of Thailand the rainy season starts in May or June. It ends in October. By then, canals and rivers have flowed together over the low fields. Mile after mile of countryside is covered by a great shallow lake.

In this water the rice crop grows. Where the water lies several feet deep, rice seed is thrown out across the fields. The rice may even be harvested by boat. Men lean over the sides of small boats and cut off the long, limp stalks just a few inches below the waterline.

In areas where the water is shallow, men and women and buffalo tramp through the water, churning up the muddy bottom. They plant the rice thickly in certain fields. When the young shoots spring up, the farmers pull them in bunches and transplant them in rows in all the flooded fields. They weed and fertilize while the fields are still flooded. As the waters go down, the rice grows tall and turns golden. It is truly gold to Thailand. For it is the biggest export crop, as well as the favorite food of the Thai (tie) people.

Harvest time comes in Thailand's coolest season. In late October the winds shift. No longer do they blow up from the southwest, bringing rain clouds from the Gulf of Thailand. Now they blow from the northeast. They bring dry, cooler air from the lands in the north. Even in this "cool" season, the temperature seldom goes below 70° on the central plain. In the northern hills, nights are cooler. They seem chilly to Thais!

The harvest season passes. In March the northeast winds warm up. They bring dry heat to most of Thailand. The rivers begin to dwindle to narrow threads of water. The canals become too shallow for boat traffic. Some of them are just mud. Fields bake and crack in the hot sun. Everyone is glad when, in May or June, the rains begin again.

Down on the long southern peninsula, the climate is different. Here the southwest winds

The Gulf of Thailand flows into the South China Sea.

bring rain from the Bay of Bengal in the west. The northeast winds bring rain clouds from the Gulf of Thailand. So rain falls on this moist, warm strip of south Thailand most months of the year. The weather is always warm, but never burning hot.

Forest and Grove

Forests cover much more than half of Thailand's acres. In the moist, warm air of the long southern peninsula, plants grow quickly. Here rain forests form a thick green tangle.

Along the seacoast big smooth mangrove trees rise from clumps of knobby roots in saltwater swamps. Inland a bit, palm trees of many kinds cluster in groves.

One palm is the rattan, as much a vine as a tree. Its leaves have barbs like claws. They fasten themselves around the trunk of a nearby tree. The slender stalk of the rattan palm climbs the other tree, clinging by its barbed leaves. This stalk is used for walking sticks. It is also split into long strips and woven into rattan furniture, or it is used as rope.

26

There are many plantations of rubber trees. The bark of each tree is slashed in a long, diagonal cut. A small cup is placed at the base of the slash. It catches the thick sap that drips down the slash. This thick sap is boiled down into sheets of crude rubber. Rubber is one of Thailand's principal products shipped abroad.

Fine big trees push up through the jungle growth. There are ebony, rosewood, and giant *mai sak,* or teak trees, which grow to be 150 feet tall.

There are thickets of bamboo in the forests, tipped with feathery green. The jointed bamboo stalks are used for building and for making paper.

Giant trees tower over workers and their carts in this forest of northern Thailand.

Ferns grow in the trees and on the banks of streams. Orchids drip from the forks of trees, and other flowers make spots of color against the dark green tangle.

Farther north, on high stony hills, grow pine and other kinds of trees that are used for lumber. Most important are the splendid teak trees with their tall straight trunks. This lumber is hard and long-lasting in any weather. It is one of the most valuable of Thailand's products.

Timber!

Scattered through the high forests of the north are the proud giant teak trees that are called *mai sak*. Their trunks stretch up straight and tall to a height of 50 or 60 feet.

"Here is a fine one," someone says.

First, it is marked for cutting. Then, workers come and cut a deep gash all the way around the tree. They cut through the growing layer, so sap cannot rise to feed the tree any longer. Slowly the giant dies and begins to dry out.

This drying out is important. After several years of drying, the wood will be light enough to float. Then the tree will be ready to be cut.

Cutting must wait until the rains soften the ground because this forest giant will fall with a huge crash. Landing on rain-softened ground, it will be less likely to be damaged.

When the giant falls, the forest trembles. Soon men swarm over the fallen tree. They slash and saw at the branches until the trunk is a long pillar, half sunk in underbrush and heaps of its own cut-off branches. It weighs several tons. How can it ever be moved?

The answer is, by elephants. Through the forest come padding two great gray elephants.

This elephant will haul out a large teak log. Elephants are careful workers in Thai forests.

Their trunks swing loosely. The men on their heads ride with folded arms. Slowly the elephants line up on one side of the log. Using trunks and bony foreheads, they push and tumble the fallen giant.

In some forests, narrow railroads have been built to help the elephants. Cranes may lift the heaviest logs. But here the elephants push the log to a huge mud-slide on a cleared slope. Down it slides to a dry streambed.

The elephants' task is over for now. The rains do the next bit of work for the lumbermen. As the streambed fills with water, the heavy log lifts and begins to float. Down to the main river it floats, bumping the banks, rasping on stones, rolling and bouncing. It sticks in the mud, and logs jam up behind it. Then along comes a gray elephant and noses it back into motion again.

Downstream, the log reaches a rafting station. Here, workmen wrap sturdy lengths of rattan around the log. They bind it firmly to a hundred others in a broad flat raft. On top of the raft they build a hut of split bamboo. In this hut the raftsmen live as the logs float downstream.

These teak logs are being assorted at the sawmill before they are cut into lumber.

A pilot watches the river in front. Men with long poles steer the raft from the back.

When the raft reaches a busier stretch of the river, it is broken up into smaller rafts. A launch tugs each one downstream to the saw-mills. There, with many a screech and groan, the huge old log is sawed into lumber. It may

31

have been four or five years since the day when it was first marked for cutting, back in the forest in the hills.

Riches Underground

Thailand has some iron, some gypsum, some lignite, and even a little lead and manganese. But its important mineral is tin. Tin is found in the hills to the southwest that stretch down the Malay Peninsula.

Tin mines are usually open pits. The topsoil is stripped away, down to the layers of earth that contain tin ore. Higher up in the hills, a dam is built to store water. Great quantities of water must be washed over the tin-bearing earth. Step by step, the lighter sand and soil are washed away. What is left behind is a black powder. When this is heated in smelters, it turns into the silvery metal we know as tin.

Tin is a valuable export. But it leaves behind the ugly gashes of the open pits. And it leaves vast sprawling heaps of leftover gray mud called tailings. Ways are now being found to treat this dead earth so that crops can grow in it.

3. Who Grew the Rice?

Who grew this fine rice?
Says the buffalo, "I.
I helped grow the rice.
For I pulled the plow
and the harrow and scraper
through deep-flooded fields.
I plowed up the mud
to a smooth bed below.
That helped, I know."

Say the women, "And we,
we helped, you can see.
With our feet in the mud
we scraped up soft beds
for the small sprouting seeds.
We helped grow the rice."

Says the scarecrow, "Me too.
I helped, yes indeed.
For I frightened off birds
from the young sprouting seeds."

Say the children, "And we,
we helped grow the rice.
We shooed out of the field
the chickens and such,
and the gray buffalo,
so the seedlings could grow."

Say the girls, "It was we
who did the transplanting,
and happily.
We swung through the fields
as if at a dance.
Our arms scooped up seedlings
with grace and with skill.
Up came roots, off went mud,
swish went the bamboo
around a fat bunch of seedlings.
Oh, yes, we helped too."

Say the young men, "We worked
with you in a long line,
the width of the field.
Three or four at a time
we poked in those seedlings.
We laughed and we joked,
and we poked in some more
till the rice was transplanted,
field after field."

"We helped the rice grow,"
say the proud drakes and ducks.
"It was not just luck
that the rice was not eaten
by insects and crabs.
Every morning by nine
we marched down in a line
to the flooded rice paddy.
We swam and we dove
and we bit and we snapped
at all the rice pests
that were nibbling. And that's
how we helped the rice grow."

"The rice grew and it grew
and turned gold in the sun.
Then through a long day
we gathered the crop
in a neighborly way.
Swish, swish went our sickles.
We held each tall stalk
to keep it from falling.
Then carefully
we laid the stalks down
in the sun to dry.
Swish, swish went our sickles
as we passed by," say the men.

Say the children, "We helped!
We kept off the rain.
With our dancing and shouting
and playing of games,
we kept the sun shining
till threshing day came."

Say the women, "And we
fixed the threshing floor.
Oh, the men did the pounding.
But we washed the ground
to make it as smooth as a stone,
to keep dust from the rice.
That was help, you must own!"

Say the men,
"We struck all the sheaves
on the hard threshing floor.
We knocked off the rice grains
till there were no more."

"We threshed too!"
say the buffalo.
"Round and around
we trampled the rice
on the threshing ground
to tramp out the grains."

"We winnowed!" cry the girls.
"We tossed up flat pans
full of rice in the breeze.
The chaff blew away.
The rice was left clean."

"If there's no wind, what then?"
say the young men.
"Then we bring out our fans
made of light bamboo.
We leap and we dance,
fanning breezes for you."

"We helped!" cry the children.
"We frightened off birds
with our slingshots and stones
and the rattle and slap
of our loud bamboo clappers.
What a great help was that!"

Then all together say,
"When the long day is done
and the carts creak away,
taking rice to the granary,
we have time to play.
By the light of bonfires
we feast and we sing.
We rejoice in the harvest
because we all know
that by working together
we made the rice grow!"

4. "Eat Rice, Eat Fish"

"Eat rice, eat fish," says a Thai villager when he speaks of having a meal. For who could have a meal without rice in Thailand? And a meal without fish is rare.

Most of the fields of Thailand are rice fields. A small ditch leads water into every field. A larger ditch feeds every small one. It gets its water in turn from a canal. And every ditch, canal, and river in Thailand always has some fish in it. Dip a hand net a few times, and you will get enough tiny silver fish, small eels, or fresh-water shrimp or rice crabs to flavor a spicy sauce called curry.

Thailand has hundreds of miles of seacoast, lined with the homes of fishermen. They make fish traps from rows of stakes in the shallows. In their boats they also take nets out into deep water. They reap rich catches of fish. Fresh and dried fish are heaped up in every marketplace.

In the north of Thailand most people eat three meals a day—morning, noon and evening. In the south and in central Thailand, they eat breakfast and a late afternoon meal with a light meal between. But all over the country, for every meal, Thais have rice, rice, rice!

Some children and adults will probably catch small fish in this klong.

In the south the rice is in fluffy white grains. In the north and northeast it is usually a special kind called "sticky rice." This rice grows in a shorter time and needs less water, so it is well suited to the north.

At every meal, too, there is a hot curry sauce with the rice. In this curry you will find some small fish or shrimp, rice crabs or dried fish, or perhaps a sharply spiced fish paste. For special meals, on holidays or at harvest time, there may be some pork, chicken, or duck.

Many farmers keep a few pigs in the open space under the house. The pigs clean up the scraps from the kitchen, which are swept down through holes in the floor. But people do not like to kill their pigs. It is against the teachings of their religion to destroy life. Instead, they cart them to market and sell them. For special feasts they buy pork from the Chinese butcher in the market.

A few chickens scratch for bugs in most farm-yards. Proud ducks march in single file to swim in the nearest canal. The children watch for nests and collect the hen and duck eggs to sell. But farmers rarely kill and eat their own poultry.

Small boat vendors are selling their products to house-wives and shopkeepers along this klong.

Sometimes a few chickens or ducks are popped into a big, loose-woven, covered basket for a trip to market. After that, they may appear in curry at some feast.

Vegetables go into the sauces too. Under the fruit trees near most village homes, you will find a vegetable garden. In the garden grow eggplant, cucumbers, lettuce, cabbage, onions, peas, corn, bamboo shoots, tomatoes, pumpkins. For spices, there are chili peppers that are hot enough to bring tears to the eyes, basil, ginger, tumeric. And garlic! Your nose tells you how popular garlic is!

43

For special feasts the men of the family will help chop vegetables and grate sweet coconuts. But the girls and their mothers prepare the everyday meals. They do their cooking on small clay stoves or in earthen fireplaces. The kitchen of a village house is usually a lean-to with one open side, so the smoke can get out easily. Extra pots can be kept in the attic of the house, just above the rafters. Cooking scraps are swept down through chinks in the floor. So the kitchen area is neat and clean.

Meals are eaten out on the veranda. This is the center of a Thai village house. The rooms are like separate little houses on three sides of the veranda, so they will catch every cool breeze. The open veranda is the living-dining room. It may also be the sleeping room for the older boys of the family. But all sleeping mats are folded up in daytime.

The furniture usually consists of sitting mats, some pillows, a cupboard or two, perhaps a sewing machine and radio, bright pictures on the walls, and a mirror. If the house has a specially big mirror, you can guess that there are teen-age daughters in the family!

Should you come for a casual visit, you would be entertained on the veranda, after you had taken off your shoes and perhaps rinsed your feet at the steps. You would be offered fruit or sweets.

If you are invited for a meal in a Thai home, you will notice that everyone gathers on the veranda. In some homes there may be a table and chairs. But in most village homes you will all sit on mats around a low tray-table. Mother and the girls place the serving bowls on the table or on the floor, as the case may be. You will

This country house has every room open to warm breezes.

be offered rice, curry, and perhaps a thin soup. You have your own small bowl, as everyone does, with a spoon. A ladle made of wood or coconut shell rests in each serving bowl.

Take your first bite carefully! This food may be "hotter" than anything you have ever tasted. Thais like it that way. Chances are you will come to like it too. You may learn to eat with your fingers instead of with a spoon. Certainly, with "rice on the land and fish in the water," as the Thais say, one need never go hungry in Thailand.

These young men are lunching in a temple courtyard where the women offer clean, tasty foods.

5. School Days

It is seven o'clock in the morning. Already the streets of Bangkok are lively. Buses by the dozen speed along, full of people going to work. Taxis dart in and out, honking their horns.

Some of the taxis are small three-wheelers. Three school children can crowd onto the seat behind the driver. In the mornings many of these "motor scooters" take boys and girls to school.

Thousands of other children are also on their way to school. Some walk with friends. Some take city buses. Some wait at the curb for school buses. Others go by boat down a canal.

Some of the boys and girls come from pretty new blue and pink and cream-colored houses on quiet lanes off main streets. Some come from flats over stores on busy avenues. Some come from old homes of brown weathered wood, with gates opening on the canals. These canals used to be Bangkok's principal roads. Some come from houseboats on the canals themselves. From all sorts of homes the schoolchildren come, early in the morning.

It seems that you are never far from a school in Thailand. Bangkok is full of them. Many are private schools where the parents pay fees. But there are also many, many government schools.

Every village has at least one big school, run by the government. Most schools used to be on the temple grounds at the edge of the villages. Now the government is building more and more of them away from the temples.

Most of the schools are built in the general shape of a **U**, occupying three sides of a central lawn. The buildings are airy and open because the weather is either warm or hot in Thailand; it is never cold. School desks are often simple ones made by the men of the village.

48

The boy spinning his top and the girls grinding rice belong to a hill tribe in northern Thailand.

You can go far south or north in Thailand. You can leave the road and climb a steep mountain path to the village of a hill tribe. The hill people seldom go down their mountain to a town. They may seldom see anyone from outside their village. The grown-ups may not even speak the Thai language. But in the village you will find a neat school with the flag of Thailand flying out in front!

Even in the villages, boys and girls generally wear uniforms to school. The boys wear neat white shirts and short khaki or blue trousers.

The girls wear neat white blouses and blue or dark red or green skirts. Everyone carries a big, heavy schoolbag full of books. Thai children buy their own books, slates, chalk, and pencils.

In the city the school day usually starts at eight in the morning. School is over at about half past two in the afternoon. This is good when the days are hot. There is time out for lunch. Some children bring food from home; others buy snacks at school. A helping of rice wrapped in a fresh green leaf makes a good lunch.

Village schools often open in the morning with flag-raising exercises at 8:00. There are classes in reading, writing, arithmetic, health, geography of Thailand, spelling, agriculture, and crafts.

From eleven to twelve o'clock there is a recess. Some children may eat lunch then. But a few will wait until they go home at three in the afternoon. They use the recess for rest and play.

At recess, one popular game is *takraw*. It is played with a ball of woven wicker about five inches in diameter. This very light ball must not be touched with the hands in play. It must be kept in motion with feet, heels, knees, arms, shoulders, or heads. This is harder than it sounds.

The school year differs from place to place in the country. It depends upon the growing season of the rice, since almost eight out of ten families make their living as rice growers. There are usually two long vacations. One is a planting vacation of four to six weeks. It comes at the beginning of the rains. Then most of the children, and teachers too, are needed to help in the wet rice fields.

Third graders in this outdoor village school learn how to multiply large sums. A student teacher instructs under the watchful eye of her supervisor.

The other is a harvest vacation. It is also four to six weeks, when the rains are over and the rice is ready to be cut. The rice seasons differ widely over the more than a thousand miles that Thailand stretches from north to south. So the school year varies too.

At the end of the school year, standard government examinations are given in all schools. If a student does not pass the examinations, he must repeat the grade. Children do not mind repeating too much because there are many different age groups in any one classroom. Many of the boys and girls start school by the time they are eight years old, but some start earlier, at seven years of age. Others wait until they are nine or ten.

All boys and girls in Thailand are supposed to have an elementary education up to the seventh grade. Then there are five years of high school to which they may choose to go. After high school, some go on to college or technical school.

6. Let's Celebrate!

The Thais use the Western calendar officially. They celebrate New Year's Day from December thirty-first through January first. They have other national holidays on the Western calendar. In April they honor the royal Chakri dynasty, the family of the King. In May they celebrate the coronation of King Bhumibol Adulyadej. In August they celebrate the Queen's birthday.

In October, on Chulalongkorn Day, they remember one of their greatest kings of a hundred years ago. They also observe United Nations Day. In December they celebrate the King's birthday.

There are school programs in all villages on national holidays, so that the people share them and feel they are a part of the nation. Often there are parades and other celebrations too. But the really festive holidays are those of the old Buddhist calendar.

Buddhism is the religion of most Thais. It is based on the teaching of a saintly man called the Buddha who lived about 600 years before Christ.

Buddhist New Year's Day

Buddhist New Year's Day comes in April. There are many ways to greet the Buddhist New Year! No wonder the celebration takes several days. The house and everything in it must be cleaned. That is an old custom adopted from India. Buddhism came from India too.

City people offer special foods to monks who may stop at their gates. City families also go to call on older relatives. They exchange special greetings. They may sprinkle scented water on one another.

Villagers have other customs of their own.

54

They take food to the Buddhist temple which is called a *wat*. There, a pleasant odor of burning incense (a sweet-smelling gum) and of flower petals fills the air. Thais take some sand to the temple, too. Each family heaps its sand up into a pointed spire. When the sand dries out and crumbles, it is swept over the courtyard to freshen it for the new year. Each grain of sand also atones for some small sin.

The Full Moon of May

The Buddha was born at the full moon of May, more than 2,500 years ago. He was born a rich Indian prince, but he was troubled by the sickness and suffering and death he saw around him. So he left his home and family and went out as a wanderer, to seek the meaning of life.

It was under a May moon, some years later, that he gained an understanding of life. The Buddha told his followers that they must always do right, without regard for reward. They must live peacefully and honorably without striving for gain, if they wished at last to reach Nirvana, the eternal peace.

Years later, when the May moon was again full, the Buddha passed from this life into Nirvana. All of these events are celebrated by Thai Buddhists at Visakha Bucha, when the moon is full in May.

This is a good time for a family to travel to one of the famous old temples on a pilgrimage. At temples holy scriptures are read. There are processions. Gifts are given. At night the temple courtyards are bright with paper lanterns and the sparkle of fireworks, under the full moon.

A Special Season

In July, when the rains have started and the days are hot and sticky, comes a special season in the Buddhist year. Every young man of Thailand tries to spend some months as a monk in a wat. Most go for the three months of the rains, when they are about twenty years of age.

56

They learn about their religion. They learn how to live a good life by being peaceful, unselfish, and thoughtful of others.

Every temple has a dormitory for monks and a special chapel in which they worship. It also has a temple for the townsfolk, where services are held at the four quarters of the moon.

Some boys go to live at the temple compound when they are as young as ten. They are called

Bangkok's Wat Arun was built on spacious grounds by the river. Known as the Temple of the Dawn, it is a favorite spot visited by many Thais.

temple boys. They help keep the dormitories clean. In the early morning they go with the monks from door to door to collect gifts of food. Temple boys go to public school, and they go home for their evening meals, since the monks do not eat after noontime. But they study and attend evening service at the wat, and sleep there.

The temple day starts before dawn. The chanting of monks is the first sound most villagers hear, even before the cocks stretch their wings and crow. By six o'clock the monks, with their orange robes covering their bowls, appear at the doors of homes. In some villages the women and girls take food to the temple and serve it there.

The rest of the day the monks spend quietly at study, rest, and worship.

Tod Kathin, Gift Day

The banks of the river are crowded with people. The windows of buildings along the shore are full of eager faces. On the water hundreds of boats jostle for space. Whole trains of boats, gay with flags and lively with music, float past, pulled by tugs.

The royal barge is anchored, awaiting the arrival of the king. The barge will lead the royal procession.

The murmur of the crowd rises to a cheer. Into sight floats the royal barge. At its prow rises a tall, proud, gilded swan's head. Along its sides flash the bright oars of dozens of rowers. In the middle of the royal boat rises the golden throne of the King himself. Other gilded boats carry the rest of the royal family.

The royal procession is on its way to some great temple on the bank of the river near Bangkok. This is *Tod Kathin* (toad kah-tin), the day when almost every family in Thailand takes gifts to some temple. The royal family leads the way in this pleasant custom.

59

Boys celebrate Tod Kathin with drums, gongs, funny masks and costumes.

Villagers prepare baskets full of gifts for the monks—sweets, notebooks, tobacco and matches, small trinkets—all tucked in around the new orange robes which are the main gift. Some people make small "trees" of bamboo with leaves of money to decorate the top of their baskets.

All over Thailand processions move through the streets, along the roads, up the canals, on their way to some temple. Boy Scout bands play while Girl Scouts in uniform march. There are decorated floats and graceful dancers and even jokesters in funny masks. Everyone enjoys Tod Kathin, gift day.

Loy Krathong, Night of Lights

Over the horizon rises a golden glow. The first curve of the full moon soon pushes up into sight behind black palm trees.

The rising moon is the signal the crowds have been waiting for. On the banks of a hundred klongs, from the steps of homes, from the sides of boats, candle flames flicker and glow. The fragrance of incense steals along on the breeze as incense sticks are lighted too.

Now out onto the waters sail a hundred thousand tiny boats. They are the *loy krathongs* (krah-tongs), "floating leaf cups." Most are made

College girls honor the holiday with a graceful dance.

of a strip of banana leaf pinned into a cup shape. Into each cup goes a candle, an incense stick, a flower or two, and perhaps small coins.

As each small flower boat is set adrift, with its candle and incense alight, a prayer may be said: "With this krathong we pay homage to the footsteps of the Lord Buddha. May it result in our happiness and render us assistance forever."

Some set their small boats adrift with a silent wish. They believe that if the candle stays alight as long as they can see the boat, the wish it carries will be granted.

The loy krathongs are a mark of respect to the Mother of Waters for her gifts to the people.

Some say they are also an apology for the water which has been soiled by use during the year.

Nowadays many people celebrate "the night of lights" mainly for fun. They go on boating parties with picnic lunches, balloons, clowns, and fireworks. Songs drift over the water as the tiny lights glow.

If you celebrate Loy Krathong at the full moon of the twelfth month of the lunar year, your wishes may all come true!

The Winter Fair

The harvest is in. Plump rice grains fill the granaries. Pumpkins are stacked in piles. The year's hardest work is finished. It is time to celebrate.

The winter fairs of olden days have now been combined with Constitution Day. Government officials make speeches. But otherwise the fairs are much the same, with booths to display the best produce and handicrafts. Prizes are given. Whole streets of wooden booths are set up. There are plays and dances and movies and exciting contests. There is plenty of fun for all.

ปุุ๋ฑ เทกระจ่าง

A Story

7. A Happy, Damp New Year

by Ramadi Vasnasong

It was shortly after dawn on the Buddhist New Year's Day when Noon, the old gardener, pushed open the gate. A drift of soft fresh air came from the canal at the foot of the garden. Birds twittered their greetings to the day. Soon, he knew, the sun would be scorching hot. For this was April in Thailand.

The old gardener arranged three low tables along the sidewalk. As he worked he mumbled to himself, "It is already five o'clock in the morning. The *Khunying* (koon-ying) will soon be out to give food to the monks."

This is an old custom. A monk may stop at your door any day with his bowl. But on special days such as New Year's Day, birthdays, wedding days, and anniversaries, special foods are prepared for the monks.

Noon did not have long to wait. Khunying, the mistress of the house, soon appeared. She wore a new skirt or *pasin* (pah-seen) and a long-sleeved blouse.

After Khunying came three maids. Each carried a tray of food which she arranged on one of the tables. There was a huge silver bowl full of steaming rice. There were packets of minced meat wrapped in fresh green banana leaves. There were mounds of fresh fruits. There were also small bunches of lotus blossoms and incense sticks.

The tables had scarcely been arranged when the first yellow-robed monk stopped in front of the gate. With bowed head and downcast eyes, he held out his bowl. Khunying put rice, a packet of minced meat, and fruit into the bowl. Last of all, on the closed lid of the bowl, she placed a bunch of flowers.

As the monk moved on, Khunying joined her

hands, raised them between her eyebrows, and bowed her head in respect.

Another monk stopped, and another. This went on until the tables were bare. Khunying then returned to the house. For she still had a full day before her.

It was not long before her eldest daughter arrived with her husband and two children— Prapun and his younger sister, Prapaisri (pra-pai-see).

Each one poured scented water on the grand-mother's hands to wash away all bad luck and purify her for the new year to come. Then they presented their gifts. Prapaisri had made a straw handbag; Prapun had chosen a piece of Thai silk and had wrapped it himself.

"You can easily tell that," said his sister. "Because the package is all lumps."

"That is not the way to start the new year," chided the grandmother with a smile. Placing her hand on the head of each child in turn, she gave her blessing and a wish for good luck.

After the ceremonies, they climbed up to a breezy room opening onto the garden. There, because it was a special day, they sat barefooted

on straw mats spread on the cool dark floor. They sipped tall glasses of chilled fruit drinks.

It was all very pleasant and quiet there, out of the hot sun. But Prapun soon got restless. Where were his cousins with their father and mother? Not until they came could the real fun begin!

Prapun rose from his mat and began to wander around the shadowy, high-ceilinged room. He stopped before a picture on one wall.

"Grandmother, why doesn't the tiger in this picture have any stripes?" he asked.

"Ah, my son," Khunying chided with a smile, "have you forgotten the old tale?"

Prapun grinned. He had not forgotten. He had heard the story many times. But he knew Khunying liked to tell it, and it was a favorite of his. Hearing it would be a good way to pass the time until the others came.

"Please tell us again," he begged.

"If you are not too restless to listen," said his grandmother, "I will tell you. Perhaps you may learn something too."

Prapun pulled his mat closer and sat down. And this was the tale his grandmother told:

How the Tiger Got His Stripes

In the olden days, the tiger had a plain yellow coat. But even then he was a fierce hunter. He could be a danger to men.

Once in those times, my heart's treasures, there was a poor old woodcutter named Mee. He earned his rice and fish by selling strips of rattan vine he was able to cut in the forest.

Working late one evening, he was startled to look around and find himself face-to-face with a fierce yellow tiger, lashing its long tail.

"I am going to eat you up," the tiger growled. And he bared his long sharp fangs.

Poor old Mee was filled with fear. There was no one nearby to call for help. If he was to escape, he must save himself. Swiftly he thought of a plan.

"Honorable sir!" he addressed the tiger. "Have you forgotten that soon there is to be a great flood? At high tide the waters will reach the clouds. The fish are going to feast on the moon and stars.

"I am cutting these rattan strips to lash my wife and children to high trees. Then they will be safe from the flood. When they are safe, I don't care what happens to me. You may eat me then, if you wish to have one last meal before the flood devours you."

As Mee told his story, the tiger began to shake with fear.

"My friend," said the tiger, "your story has greatly disturbed me. I will spare your life if you in turn will save me from the flood by lashing me to a tree also. I cannot swim, you see. Therefore I am very much afraid of water."

70

The old woodcutter tried not to look too pleased. His plan had worked!

"Very well, friend tiger," he said. "Stand here while I wind my rattan strips around your paws and lift you to safety."

The tiger stood still. The old woodcutter tied him up tight. And then, my children, he gave him such a beating that it went down in tiger history.

From that time to this, all tigers bear the marks of that beating in stripes down their sides. And old Mee is remembered for his quick wits. So, my heart's treasure, we come to the end of our story of "How the Tiger Got His Stripes."

Just as Khunying finished her story, voices were heard in the garden.

"Aha!" cried Prapun. "I hear Cousin Tiger coming. Let me tie you safely to a tree, dear friend, while I wish you luck in the coming year!"

Soon the young people were all armed with bowls of water. They threw water upon one another until all were soaking wet. For that is the way to celebrate the New Year in traditional Thai style.

"Perhaps the young people forget some of the old religious feeling of the holiday," said Khunying with a smile. "But their wits are as quick as those of old woodcutter Mee. Also, it is April, and the weather is hot. So why not cool off?"

From her slender fingertips she tossed a few drops of scented water at her eldest son, father of the newly arrived young people. He looked a bit surprised!

8. Past and Present

The Happy Land of Gold

In the long-ago times, so we are told in an old tale, the world belonged to the gods. But even they did not always live in peace. Between Indra, the Rain God, and the Demon of Drought a bitter feud long raged. Indra tried to keep the earth cool and fresh and green with showers. The Demon of Drought tried to bake it dry.

At last in a great battle the Rain God defeated the Demon of Drought. This victory meant that where the battle-ax of the Demon fell to earth, there would always be plenty of showers. This happy spot was named The Land of Gold.

73

In later ages, men came down from the north to live in the green valleys of the Land of Gold. But still the Rain God continued to visit it, to frolic there with his band of cloud nymphs. Uma, the Goddess of Earth, watched tenderly over it. And the Land of Gold, which we know today as Thailand, continued to be a happy place.

Out of China

Thailand does not have a very long history. Twelve hundred years ago the Thais were a tribe living in Yunnan province in south China. At this time a brave warrior chieftain named Piloko (pea-lo-ko) appeared. It was under him that the Thai people prospered and grew into a nation.

As the Thais grew in number, they began to spread out. Small groups wandered over the hills and drifted down river valleys. Some went westward, down into the valley of the mighty Irrawaddy River and the Salween into what is now Burma. Some went down the Mekong River to the east, into the lands that are now Laos, Vietnam, and Cambodia. There are still Thais living in all these countries.

All over this area, tribes are still on the move. Many of the hill tribes of northern Thailand have lived in the country only a generation or two. They came from Laos or Cambodia or Burma or down from China. There are many thousands of people who are not Thais living in Thailand today.

In 1253 the homeland of the Thais in China was captured by Kublai Khan and his armies. It was then that most of the Thai people moved south, down the broad valley of the Menam Chao Phraya, and founded the country of Siam.

The War of the White Elephants

This was a time in history when there were few strong nations in the world. In Europe as well as in Asia, there were many many kings and princes who ruled over small kingdoms and principalities. Each ruler had an army. And it seemed there was fighting going on most of the time.

So it was in Siam. The Thais fought the people who had been living in their valley. They fought the once strong kingdom of the Khmers

to the east. They fought the kings of Burma
to the west.

Sometimes Siam had a strong ruler. Under
one of these men they seized the Khmers'
beautiful capital city of Angkor. Sometimes they
had weak rulers. Then they were invaded in
turn. It did not take much in those days to
start a war.

Once a King of Pegu, in Burma, coveted the
white elephants of the King of Siam. Since
white elephants were very rare and difficult to
find, the King of Pegu sent an army to capture
some of those belonging to the Siamese ruler.
This fight is called the "War of the White
Elephants." But it was really a very small war.

The Kingdom of Ayudhaya

In the early 1600's, the capital of Siam was the rich and beautiful city of Ayudhaya (ah-you-dah-ya). At this time the Portuguese, the Dutch, the English, and the French were competing for the rich trade with the Spice Islands and the Orient. Ships from the West found their way to the ports of Siam. The King made them welcome. Siam even sent men to visit courts in Europe.

Some of the Europeans tried to turn the people away from the religion of Buddha toward their religion. Others used armed force to further their trade and their power. These difficulties caused foreign trade to dwindle.

The end of the greatness of Ayudhaya came at about this same time. Dissatisfied nobles broke away and set themselves up as rulers on their own. Outsiders saw that the country was weak. The armies of Burma nibbled at the western and southern borders of Siam. At last they marched boldly in and sacked Ayudhaya itself, about 200 years ago.

Up from the Depths

What a sight! Temples and palaces were in ruins. The homes of Ayudhaya were ablaze. Her people lay dead in the streets. Siam seemed lost.

One general did manage to escape with 500 followers. They were not ready to give up. They founded a new town on a curve of the Menam. From it they drove the Burmese out of the country.

A few years later they started a new capital

across the waters of the Menam. It was called Bangkok. It is still the capital and principal city of the land. And the family of the king who founded the city is still on the throne.

This new family of kings, the Chakri Dynasty, encouraged trading with foreign countries. In small boats the visitors from Europe came up the shallow river to the river gate of the Grand Palace of the King. Big ships had to wait outside sandbars in the river.

The traders found that all Siamese bowed to the ground at the sight of their King. Slaves by the hundreds ran to do his royal bidding. The Kings of Siam were all-powerful in those days.

In 1868 King Chulalongkorn came to the Siamese throne. He had been educated in European ways. He abolished slavery. He sent young men of Siam, including several of his sons, abroad to learn more about the world outside.

As more and more of these educated young men came back from schooling abroad, they wanted to help govern their country. They were dissatisfied because the people of Siam had very little voice in the government.

The Royal Palace in Bangkok looks like the setting for a modern fairy tale.

At last, in 1932, a group of young men wrote a constitution and forced the King to accept it. Since then Siam, now called Thailand, has been a constitutional monarchy.

Thailand Today

To most people of Thailand, their own village is most important. The priest or abbot of the temple, or *wat,* at one end of the village is one of its most respected men. The other leading man is the headman, chosen by the villagers.

The headman keeps track of births and deaths in the village. He takes care of streets and roads. He chooses men to look after the irrigation ditches.

The irrigation men can call on villagers to work when help is needed. The villagers are used to working together. They work in one another's fields at planting and harvesting time.

The headman meets with other village headmen in a commune made up of nearby villages. One of the headmen is chosen leader of the commune. He attends a meeting once a month in the district office. He goes home and tells his people what he has learned there.

The modernization of Thailand's monarchy is honored on Constitution Day. Crowds celebrate the day with many bright decorations.

There is a district officer in charge of each district. He is sent out from the central government in Bangkok. The district officer is the government official the villagers know best. He collects taxes, runs the local governments, and acts as a sort of judge.

A number of districts make up a province. There are 70 provinces called *changwats* (chung-wuts) in the nation of Thailand. Each province has a governor appointed by the national government.

The villagers and city people vote for members of the parliament, which is the National Assembly. The prime minister is the active head of the government.

Most people in Thailand are not much concerned about government, though. And, as long as the king is on his throne, as long as the pointed spires of the temples reach toward the sky, as long as there is water in the canals and rice grows in the fields, the people of Thailand are content.

A Story

9. The Golden Serpent Barge

by Ramadi Vasnasong

The royal boat races were over for another year. The family car was inching its way through jammed streets, noisy with the honking of horns. Prapun whistled as a darting motor scooter whizzed into the path of a crowded bus, then zipped safely aside.

"That reminds me of the race," he said. "Do you remember when the princess' boat almost nicked the golden serpent on the royal barge?"

"Yes," said his sister, Prapaisri. "That was too close!"

"I wonder what would happen," said Prapun,

"if anyone did hit that golden serpent?"

"I can tell you what would have happened in the old days, when the King had power of life and death," said Khunying, his grandmother. "In those days a boatman who damaged the royal barge was beheaded!"

"Really?" cried Prapun. "Did they really do it, Grandmother?"

"Have you never heard the story of Pun Tai Norasing?" his grandmother asked. "It is a tale you should know." This is the story she told:

The Faithful Boatman

It happened several hundred years ago, when Ayudhaya was the capital of Siam, that the King who ruled in those days was very fond of sports. Best of all he liked boxing, and next best, boat racing.

One day, the King heard that there was to be a temple fair at Wat Nampu, with both boxing and boat racing. He ordered a barge brought around.

"Not the royal barge!" he commanded. "We shall visit the fair in disguise."

So off went the king and his men, manning the oars like a troop of village lads. At the fair they mingled with the crowd. Part of the temple grounds had been roped off for boxing matches. The judge was beating a gong and announcing, "This well-known boxer will meet any comer in the ring!"

"I accept the challenge!" cried the King. He leaped into the ring, dancing and twirling about to limber up his muscles. In the middle of the second round, the King was able to knock out the local hero. As the crowd cheered, the King left the ring, unrecognized.

"Now for the boat races," said he.

In the race for the grand prize, the King was impressed by the skill of one boatman. He took the boatman back to Ayudhaya and made him Commander of the Royal Barges, with the title of Pun Tai Norasing.

What journeys they had then, the King and his favorite boatman! Up the river, down the *klong,* skimmed the royal barge, skillfully steered by Pun Tai Norasing. The King seldom rode his royal elephants any more.

One day at the season of high water, the King decided to go fishing. Pun Tai Norasing was at the helm of the royal barge. The current was very swift that day, and the river was narrow and twisting. A sudden eddy of current caught the prow of the barge. Despite all that Pun Tai Norasing could do, the prow struck a low-hanging branch of a tree. To the horror of all, the golden prow snapped off and fell into the water.

Leaping ashore, the boatman sank to his knees.

"I beg of Your Majesty," he said, "to build here a shrine and place on it my head, my sword, and the prow of the boat."

Nonsense!" said the King. "This was no fault of yours. Let us forget this accident."

"No, Your Majesty," insisted Pun Tai Norasing. "This is the law of the land. If you let me live, against the law, my name will be disgraced. And the citizens will lose respect for Your Majesty's authority."

"Let me make a clay figure," the King suggested. "We can give it your title, Pun Tai Norasing, and cut off its head."

Pun Tai Norasing only smiled. He would not agree.

So the shrine was built. On it were placed the broken prow of the royal barge and the sword and head of the faithful boatman who valued his honor and the King's law more than life itself.

10. Made in the Village

The houses of this village look like those of most villages. They have warm, brown walls of wood and plaited bamboo. They are raised up on poles. But their yards look like beds of giant flowers. Each flower is a bright-painted paper parasol.

The people of this village have rice fields. They raise fruits and vegetables. But they also have a village industry—making paper parasols.

In one yard we see bamboo frames with spokes poking out like the legs of giant spiders. Nearby, in a shady spot, young men glue layers of paper onto the frames. When the glue is dry, the paper is painted—yellow, pink, blue, or black.

The flowers we see tilted to the sun are freshly painted parasols set out to dry. When they are dry, artists dip their brushes into paint. Swish, swish, under their brushes bright flowers swiftly appear on the parasols.

Last of all, the frames are folded down. A paper ring is slipped over each to hold it snug. Then off to the cooperative the parasols go.

All the villagers belong to an organization called a marketing cooperative. By selling their goods together, they get a better price for their

Freshly painted umbrellas drying in the sun look like giant flowers.

work. This marketing cooperative ships the goods far and wide for sale.

You may see a woman strolling down a sunny road in Burma or Indonesia or Malaysia under a painted paper parasol from north Thailand.

In a nearby village, paper is made. Bamboo fibers are cooked to a thin "soup." Wooden frames, something like window screens with fine net instead of metal screen, are dipped into the "soup." When the net is coated, the frames are propped up to dry in the sun. The coating dries to a thin sheet of soft paper, which is pulled away from the frame.

Using a blowtorch, this silversmith helps design a silver ash tray.

Expert weavers show that it is easy to make straw baskets.

Still another village has silversmiths. They warm sheets of silver over small charcoal fires. When the silver is soft, they pound it into bowls and other shapes. With great skill, they pound out flowers and the forms of animals, gods, and men around the sides of the bowls.

In one village, boxes, bowls, and plates are finished with shining smooth lacquer in black and gold. It is surprising how lightweight these boxes are. They are woven of fine bamboo. The bamboo is covered with layers of lacquer.

Lac is a sort of black sticky gum found on *rac* trees. Lacquer is made from it.

91

Brilliant colors make Thai silks popular. Here is the
spinning room of a small factory.

When the surface of a box or bowl is smooth
and shining, an artist paints on the black with
gold paint. He works swiftly but with great care.

In other villages there are weaving shops with
spinning wheels and rows of looms. Some weave
cotton goods. In others the famous Thai silks
are woven with bright and lively colors. More
and more of this beautiful cloth is being sold in
other lands.

Thailand has a large number of village
industries. Men in many homes weave baskets
for sale. Many shops sell nothing but baskets.
Some baskets are deep with small necks. Fishers

in the canals wear these to hold their catch. Shallow, scoop-shaped baskets are used for scooping in some fish.

Market people sell all sorts of foods from wide, flat basket trays. Chickens and ducks are carried to market in big, loose-woven, covered baskets. Many homes have walls of bamboo mats woven like baskets. And everyone has basket-woven floor mats. There are also the light, cool straw hats woven like baskets.

In some homes, girls make torches, brooms, and fans of bamboo and palm leaves. They make ladles from coconut shells for serving food.

Weavers look out of their windows to see how the dyed silk is drying.

From almost every home, it seems, some girl or woman goes to the early morning market in the town nearby with something to sell. It may be a tray of fruit, a few bunches of onions, or some silvery fish still shining wet.

Paddling her small *sampan*, the market woman soon finds herself in a traffic jam of small, loaded boats. But everyone is cheery. No one is in a hurry. There is time to visit and, perhaps, to have a snack from a restaurant boat, as well as time to buy and to sell. With luck, there will be a few coins to take home.

There are not many factories in Thailand. The big stores and businesses are mainly owned by Thais of Chinese ancestry. But the Thais, with their homecrafts and market gardens, add a little cash income to the living the rice crop brings.

A Story

11. The Spirits of the Klongs

Lallana shivered as she stepped out onto the porch of her home. Early morning mists curled up from the waters of the *klong* like soft gray plumes. She thought they looked like the spirits of the klong, rising up to hide from the bright sunlight.

The spirits! Lallana glanced at the small house which stood on its pole at a corner of the porch. Yes, her mother had filled the small bowl with rice. The tiny vase had a fresh flower. At the doorway of the spirit house stood the small china man and woman put there to wait upon the spirits. Outside the house were a tiny china dog and cow. They were there for the spirits too. Yes, the spirits had everything to make them content. Lallana brought her hands together at her forehead. She bowed a good morning to the spirits of the place. Then she squatted down on the steps to wash her face in the water of the klong.

A *sampan* sped past with a shiny motor chugging at its stern. It sent small wavelets splashing up the steps. The wavelets pushed Lallana's own small sampan softly against the steps—knock, knock, knock.

"Are you tired of being tied to the steps, good sampan?" Lallana asked silently.

"Knock, knock," said the sampan in reply.

"Very well," said Lallana. "Let us go for a journey, you and I—and Baby Brother."

For here came Baby Brother, teetering on his fat legs. His arms were spread wide. He smiled all over his round face.

Lallana stepped down onto the flat stern of her boat. She held out her arms to Baby Brother. Soon he was settled between her knees as she crouched over her paddle. She slipped

the loop of rope holding the boat over the top
of its post.

Mother came out on the porch with a basin
heaped with clothes to wash in the canal.

"Ho, child!" Mother called. "Wait a moment!"
She vanished into the dim house.

"Take this *baht*," she said a moment later,
reappearing. She handed a crisp piece of paper
money to Lallana. "Bring me some ginger root
from the market."

Lallana tucked the baht note into her pocket.
With a wave of her hand she was off, paddling
swiftly down the klong. From his snug seat
between her knees, Baby Brother waved too.

Where a side klong flowed into her canal, Lallana saw some children on the bank. They had fishnets on long handles. They dipped the nets into the water, and they waited a long, slow moment. Then they pulled up the nets and peered down among the wet meshes at the bottom. Sometimes there was the flash of silver from a tiny fish or two. They popped the fish into the small deep baskets they wore at their waists.

The smallest boy looked sad. He dipped his net. He pulled it up. Down again. Up again. But there was no fish. The corners of his mouth drooped lower and lower as Lallana watched.

Shifting Baby Brother, Lallana leaned forward. She found the fishnet that she kept in her boat. Swiftly she dipped it over the side of the boat. For a long moment she waited, watching the still water. When she thought she saw a flash of silver, she pulled up sharply. Into the boat flipped the wet net. Down in the bottom lay two small silver fish, as big as her longest finger. There was one tiny eel, slim as a blade of grass.

The small boy on the bank was lifting his net again. One tear trembled in the corner of his eye, ready to trickle down beside his button nose. Lallana reached into her net. She scooped the two fish and the one eel up into her hand. She flung them into the small boy's net.

"There, small fisherman! Those are yours," she called as she paddled on.

Sometimes Lallana paddled close to the banks. Plantations of big-leaved banana trees and spindly betel nut palms made deep shade there. The air stroked her cheek like the cool fingers of kindly spirits.

Sometimes she paddled out into the middle of the stream. There the sunshine lay like a warm hand on her shoulders.

She paddled under a tall wooden bridge, with steps up each side to make it high enough for a *rua,* a cargo boat loaded with sacks of rice, to go under.

Up on the bridge stood an old man. He leaned on the railing and watched the boats go by. He looked lonely.

"Good morning, Honorable Grandfather," called Lallana, raising her hands to her forehead in respectful greeting. She clapped her Baby Brother's small hands together in greeting too.

The old man looked down and smiled. He returned their greeting. Then Lallana paddled on, turning down another canal toward the market klong.

Now the traffic was thicker. The sun was high. The canal was full of market boats. Some boats were heaped with papayas, yellow-green of skin, thick with sweet orange-colored flesh inside. Some were heaped with shaggy brown coconuts, or bristly green pineapples. Some had loads of betel nuts like hard green lemons in bunches, or sugarcane in long, jointed stalks, dripping with sweet juice. There were boatloads of potatoes, with bunches of onions, green and white, on top.

The market women paddled along, in their dark blouses and trousers, with high cool hats of straw, shaped like lampshades. They sold hens' eggs, vegetables, fresh or dried fish, bananas, and bunches of bright flowers.

Looking at some flowers, Lallana almost bumped into a boat full of sweets on flat trays. Each tray was under a cap of netting to keep insects away. She would like some sweets, Lallana thought. So would Baby Brother. Her hand went to her pocket where the baht note rustled at a touch. Ginger root! That was what she was to buy, she remembered with a start.

Lallana looked all about her for a boat with

twisty brown ginger roots. But now, down the middle of the canal, came a houseboat. She had to paddle aside to get out of its way.

The man of the family was poling the boat, with one end of the long pole against his chest, the other end deep in the river mud.

The woman of the family was bent over her charcoal burner, blowing at the flame. The baby slept in his hammock, swinging softly with the motion of the boat.

Under the rounded cover of the boat, Lallana could see bedding neatly stacked and kitchen tools hanging from the walls. What fun to live on a houseboat, Lallana thought to herself.

At the stern of the boat, as it swept past her, Lallana saw a small boy playing with a wooden toy. While she watched, a cat jumped down from the roof of the houseboat where it had been lying in the sun. It brushed the small boy's arm. His toy fell into the canal with a splash!

The small boy looked surprised. Before he could cry out, Lallana paddled to the spot and fished up the floating toy. She tossed it up to him. It landed with a plunk beside the boy.

"There, Small Brother! Do not cry!" called

Lallana as she paddled smoothly on.

"That was a good deed, Small Woman!" called the father, resting on his pole.

Lallana meant to buy the ginger root then and head for home. The sun was high now. Many of the market boats were almost empty. But there was still so much to see!

Now as Lallana paddled on, the canal widened out. Instead of small open-fronted shops, there were bigger buildings on the banks. One was a rice warehouse. A row of ruas, the curve-topped cargo boats, were drawn up alongside the warehouse dock. Lines of coolies trotted up sloping gangplanks to the boats. Then back they trotted to the warehouse, bent under heavy rice sacks.

Another huge open shed housed a boat builder. Lallana sniffed the sharp smell of fresh-sawed wood. She saw in the shadows long, thick, greenish teak logs. She saw men at work in pairs, swaying forward and backward to the rhythm of a crosscut saw. She heard hammers and the clatter of other tools as men shaped long planks to the curve of a boat keel.

Lallana stayed, watching the boat builders, until Baby Brother began to whimper. He was

hungry, of course. And she had no food for him.

"Oh, young friend," said a voice above her. Lallana looked up. The houseboat with the small boy was beside her. It was the boy's mother who spoke. "Will you have some rice and curry?"

She handed down to Lallana a steaming bowl. The bowl was heaped with rice. Over the rice was a tasty sauce with vegetables and tiny pink shrimps. Baby Brother could hardly wait to get his fingers into the bowl! Between them they soon licked it clean.

"Thank you," said Lallana, handing back the empty bowl.

"No thanks to me," smiled the mother. "One good deed sown, another reaped."

104

Now Lallana noticed that the sun was dropping behind the tall trees. Where had the day gone? She must hurry home to reach it before dark!

Swiftly she paddled back up the klong, past the rice warehouse, back to the marketplace. It was quiet now, at day's end. All the fruit and vegetable boats were gone. And still she had no ginger root.

On the steps before one of the open-fronted shops, two men sat taking their ease.

"Please, good fathers," said Lallana, "where can I buy some ginger root?"

"Ginger root!" said one man with a laugh. "We sell only silks and cottons here."

"Let me ask my wife," said the other man.

He called back into the shadows, and soon out stepped a pretty young woman with a small parcel wrapped in a fresh square of banana leaf.

"Here is your ginger root, young lady," said the man, handing the parcel down to Lallana.

"Oh, thank you," she said, putting the baht note into his hand.

Then off she paddled, faster than ever. For a rosy stain filled the western sky. And darkness comes swiftly in the tropics.

Soon Lallana must turn off into a side canal. But which one was it? It would have a tall-backed bridge, she remembered. But there was a bridge, it seemed, on every canal! Lallana began to feel a lump in her middle.

"Ho, young friend!" she heard a voice call.

Dragging her paddle, she swung about. On the top of a high bridge down a canal beside her stood an old man. He had been there in the morning. Now he waved and called again.

"This is your way home, young friend!"

So up the side canal Lallana paddled.

Now from houses along the canal, lamplight streamed out in warm golden lines. Lallana could see families seated on floor mats, having their evening meal. She could hear the music of unseen radios. The homes looked so safe and bright and comfortable. How she wished that she were home!

At one of the houses a girl stepped out to dip some water from a big rainwater storage jar. She looked like one of the children who had been fishing in the canal in the morning. Now, through the doorway, she could see the small boy to whom she had given the fish. He was squatting in the lamplight, dipping his fingers into a food bowl.

"I hope his mother has mashed my small fish into a good fish paste for his rice tonight," Lallana said to herself. She smiled. For now she knew she was nearly home.

On she paddled wearily. The slap of the paddle as it cut the water sounded strange in the darkness. The whisper of ghostly spirit voices rustled among the dark trees. Baby Brother sagged heavily against her, fast asleep.

Lallana was so tired that she almost paddled past the familiar steps of home. But just as she reached the porch, a lamp came bobbing out the door. She heard her father's voice.

"I will take the boat and look for them," he was saying.

As he moved toward his sampan, Lallana's smaller one bumped the steps.

"Here we are, Father!" Lallana called.

Lallana's mother tossed more rice husks into her small clay stove. The flame glowed brighter. Soon Lallana's fingers were busy with a bowl of hot, delicious rice and sauce.

"How did you find your way in the dark?" Mother asked as she unwrapped the ginger root.

"It was the spirits of the klong," said Lallana, with a small bow toward the spirit house outside. "The good spirits brought us safely home."

Index

109

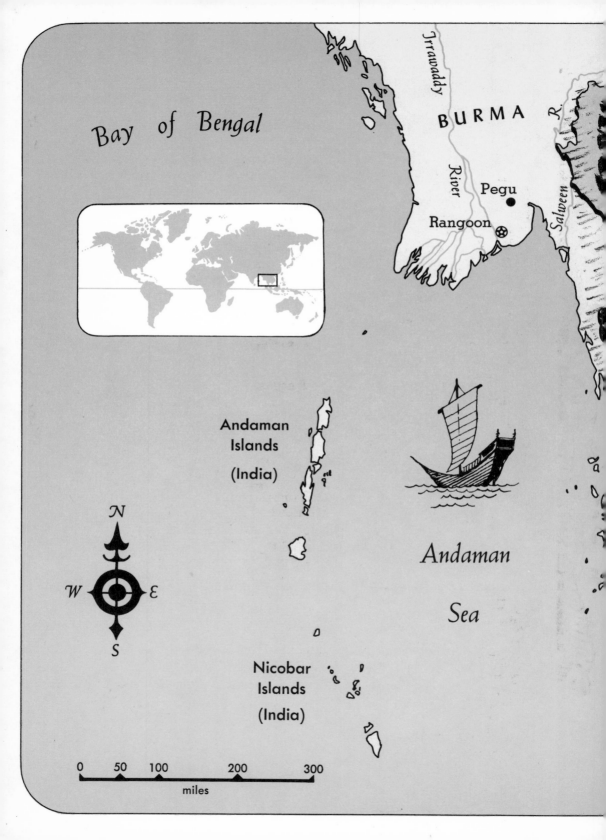